Unrugged Individualism

Unrugged Individualism
The Selfish Basis of Benevolence

David Kelley

Institute for Objectivist Studies
Poughkeepsie, New York

ISBN 1-57724-000-6

Second printing, October 1996

Printed in the United States of America

Institute for Objectivist Studies
82 Washington Street, Suite 207
Poughkeepsie, New York 12601

Contents

Acknowledgments

I want to thank the following people who provided invaluable commentary, criticism, and suggestions for improvement of this essay: Larry Abrams, David Axel, Neera Kapur Badhwar, Nathaniel Branden, Roger Donway, Marsha Enright, Donald Heath, Stephen Hicks, Lester Hunt, James Lennox, Kenneth McLaughlin, and David Ross.

1 Introduction

When Howard Roark first goes to see Steven Mallory, in Ayn Rand's novel *The Fountainhead*, Roark finds the sculptor in a state of semi-drunken despair, his idealism battered by the conformity, cynicism, and vulgarity he sees around him. When Mallory discovers that Roark's idealism is genuine but unbattered, he breaks down, sobbing, and Roark offers solace.

> After a while Mallory sat up. He looked at Roark and saw the calmest, kindest face — a face without a hint of pity. It did not look like the countenance of men who watch the agony of another with a secret pleasure, uplifted by the sight of a beggar who needs their compassion; it did not bear the cast of the hungry soul that feeds upon another's humiliation. Roark's face seemed tired, drawn at the temples, as if he had just taken a beating. But his eyes were serene and they looked at Mallory quietly, a hard, clean glance of understanding — and respect.[1]

Roark's kindness to Mallory, marked by "understanding and respect" rather than any "secret pleasure" at the latter's agony, is portrayed as a genuine virtue. It is a moving scene of *benevolence* between human beings, one of many that occur in Rand's novels. "Benevolence" means good will toward others. It is a positive attitude toward people in general, a desire for their well-being and for peaceful, cooperative relationships with them. It is contrasted with hostility, malice, envy, or other forms of malevolence. It includes such traits as kindness, generosity, sympathy, charity, and tolerance as elements. (In moral philosophy, these latter are sometimes called the "virtues of benevolence.") The author of *The Fountainhead* and of *Atlas Shrugged* clearly regarded benevolence as a positive trait, an element in the proper relationships among men.

Yet the author of "The Objectivist Ethics," and of other essays that presented the moral code of Objectivism in nonfiction terms, never gave this trait the kind of emphasis and attention she devoted to virtues like rationality, productiveness, and justice. Rand wrote an essay on one aspect of benevolence, the help one should give to strangers in an emergency,[2] but neither she nor any of her followers and interpreters produced a systematic philosophical analysis of benevolence in general, as an everyday attitude toward living with other people in society.

Such an analysis would have to address the following basic questions:

- What is the relationship between benevolence and altruism? Since the Objectivist ethics rejects altruism as a moral principle, Objectivists cannot advocate benevolence without distinguishing it clearly from altruism. How is this distinction to be drawn?

- What is the relationship between benevolence toward others and the benevolent view of the universe (or the benevolent sense of life), which Rand discusses in her writings on aesthetics? As we will see, this is a key question for our understanding of benevolence.

- What is the status of benevolence in the Objectivist ethics? How is it to be defined as a virtue? How does it relate to the primary values and virtues that Objectivism endorses? Is it a major virtue or a minor one?

- What are the elements of benevolence? What specific kinds of actions does it require of us in dealing with others?

Rand did address the first of these questions, concerning benevolence and altruism. She argued that altruism is *not* the basis of good will toward others, and in fact is incompatible with it. Yet if we do not have answers to the other questions on the list, benevolence remains a kind of afterthought, a neglected virtue, in the Objectivist ethics. Such neglect has consequences. It contributes to the perception of Objectivism as a cold and even a cruel doctrine of "rugged" individualism. The critics who accuse Rand of advocating the greedy pursuit of one's own gain at the expense of others are grossly misrepresenting her views. But the misrepresentation sticks because the Objectivist critique of altruism has been much more prominent than the Objectivist defense of benevolence.

There have also been consequences for Objectivists themselves. As guidance in dealing with other people, the moral code of Objectivism stresses the virtue of justice, and especially the necessity for moral judgment. It has not given equal emphasis to the positive, outgoing, benevolent attitude that ought to be an important part of a life-affirming philosophy. As a result, many Objectivists feel alienated from the people around them, keenly aware of their faults but not their potential for good, more comfortable pulling weeds than making the flowers grow.

This essay addresses such problems by offering the first comprehensive Objectivist analysis of benevolence. Chapter 2 examines the relationship between benevolence and altruism, contrasting Ayn Rand's view with that of conventional morality and posing the question whether benevolence is a major or a minor virtue. Chapter 3 examines the relationship between benevolence and the "benevolent view of the universe." Benevolence toward others is often seen as a response to failure, suffering, and loss on their part — a response to negative features of life and thus a minor virtue from the standpoint of the benevolent view of the universe. I will show, however, why benevolence is essentially a commitment to achieving a positive value, and why it is a major virtue, comparable in many respects to productiveness. My reasons for this conclusion are provided in Chapters 4-7, which explain the importance of benevolence in obtaining the benefits derivable from other people. In Chapters 8-10, finally, I will discuss civility, sensitivity, and generosity as important components of benevolence.

2 Benevolence and altruism

Benevolent actions are typically regarded as altruistic, both in conventional morality and in the writings of most philosophers. This common view may be summarized as follows: Benevolence involves a concern for the well-being of others rather than one's own. Sometimes we provide benefits to others in exchange for, or as a means to, things that benefit ourselves. In distinction from such acts, genuine benevolence is supposed to involve an unselfish disposition to care for and help another person for his own sake—in pursuit of *his* good, not ours. In this respect, moreover, the common view holds that benevolence is the quintessentially moral act, on the altruist assumption that the essence of morality is service to others.[3] Thus a benevolent act such as helping an elderly woman to cross a street is a "good deed," a source of moral pride, in a way that other common actions—going to work in the morning, reading a novel, getting the children ready for school—are not.

This common view, then, incorporates the following three assumptions:

(1) As a doctrine, altruism is true; as a practice it is virtuous.

(2) The virtues of benevolence are altruistic, not self-interested.

(3) The virtues of benevolence are of major importance in morality.

5

As a point of departure in our analysis of benevolence, let us review what Rand and other Objectivist writers have said about each of these assumptions.

Assumption (1) is obviously incompatible with the egoistic ethics of Objectivism. Rand held that the ultimate value is one's own life and happiness; that all other values, including the values involved in our relationships with others, are means to this end; and that the purpose of morality is to help us achieve the end by identifying the kinds of goals, actions, and traits of character required for our survival as human beings. "Man must choose his actions, values, and goals by the standard of that which is proper to man—in order to achieve, maintain, fulfill and enjoy that ultimate value, that end in itself, which is his own life."[4]

She rejected altruism as a principle of self-sacrifice, a principle that says the goal of our actions should be to benefit others rather than ourselves. "The basic principle of altruism is that man has no right to exist for his own sake, that service to others is the only justification of his existence, and that self-sacrifice is his highest moral duty, virtue, and value."[5] By this definition, the paradigm of altruism is complete self-immolation, as in the story of Jesus, who died to atone for the sins of mankind; or the martyrdom of the Christian saints; or the demands of totalitarian leaders in this century that their citizens sacrifice their freedom, prosperity, and even their lives for the good of the nation.

The term "altruism" is rarely understood as requiring this extreme sort of self-sacrifice, and Rand has been criticized for attacking a straw man. Philosophers typically use the term "altruism" to refer to any act that is "other-regarding," directed to the good of another, leaving open the possibility a) that we may properly act for our own benefit on other occasions, or b) that even altruistic acts may also serve our own interests without losing their altruistic character.[6] But a closer look will reveal that on any plausible understanding of the term, altruism does involve self-sacrifice and is thus incompatible with egoism.

Possibility (a) is expressed in the conventional idea that we have to apportion our time between the things we do for ourselves and the things we do for others. Insofar as the things we do for others are assumed to be in conflict with our own interest, or to take time away from the pursuit of our interest, then they cannot be justified by an ultimate standard that is egoistic. A commitment to one's own life and happiness, Rand observed, is a full-time job. Any action not serving that end is at least a mild form of self-sacrifice, a use of our time and effort for things that do not benefit us, or that provide a lesser benefit than we might obtain by other uses of our resources.

Possibility (b) assumes that our interests need not conflict with those of other people, so that a single action, a single use of our time and effort, may serve both our ends and theirs. But the question still arises: which end is ultimate? Is the ultimate intended beneficiary of my action myself or the other person? Objectivism holds that the agent should be the ultimate intended beneficiary of his own actions, helping others only when their good is a means to his own, or an ingredient in it (a constitutive means), as in a close personal relationship. Genuine altruism, by contrast, presumably requires that the other person be the ultimate intended beneficiary of at least some actions — that we act for his sake, as an end in itself. And this implies a willingness to act for his sake even if it did *not* serve our interests. Rand was therefore not attacking a straw man. She was attacking the principle of altruism in terms of its essence, its demand that we treat ourselves as means to the ends of others, even if not every advocate of the principle is prepared to accept it in full.

This discussion of altruism, however, leaves open the question of whether benevolence is altruistic — the question raised by assumption (2). Altruism gains much of its tenacity as an element in conventional morality from the assumption that there are regular and widespread conflicts of interest among individuals. On that assumption, pursuing my own self-interest requires that I adopt an aggressive, competitive policy toward others, seeking my advantage at their expense, exploiting their weaknesses, and—in the extreme case, if I think I can get away with it—employing force and fraud against them. If I refrain from such actions, if I treat others benevolently, then on that assumption my action can only be construed as a sacrifice of my own interests for their benefit. For this reason, many people associate benevolence with altruism.

But Rand rejected the assumption that the interests of rational people conflict in any fundamental sense. The objective values required by our nature, the values that underlie our specific interests, require that we seek peaceful, productive, cooperative relationships with others; that we deal with others by trade, exchanging value for value, rather than by plunder and predation. Trade is a principle of justice, which Rand considered to be a cardinal virtue. Insofar as benevolence means a commitment to behaving peacefully toward others, respecting their rights and giving them what is due, it is an issue of justice, which is a selfish virtue, not an act of altruism.

Rand also recognized a role for benevolence in the sense of extending positive help. In "The Ethics of Emergencies," she says that the help we give to people whom we value is not a sacrifice. To use her example, a husband who spends a fortune to find a cure for his wife's illness is not engaged in sacrifice, assuming that he values her well-being above any other use of his money. "The proper method of judging when or whether one should help another person is by reference to one's own rational self-interest and one's own hierarchy of values: the time, money or effort one gives or the risk one takes should be proportionate to the value of the person in relation to one's own happiness."[7] This, she says, is an issue of integrity—of acting to preserve the things one values—and integrity, like justice, is a selfish virtue.

Finally, as a kind of limiting case, help to strangers is appropriate in emergencies, on the basis of "the generalized respect and good will which one should grant to a human being in the name of the potential value he represents...."[8] Even in this context, then, the Objectivist ethics tells us to act as value-seekers, pursuing our rational, long-term self-interest. Benevolence, to the extent that it is appropriate, is not altruistic.

Going further, Objectivists have argued that altruism is *incompatible* with genuine benevolence. If self-esteem is an objective human need, then we cannot see ourselves as means to the ends of others—we cannot accept the premise that someone else's need is a moral claim on our efforts and resources, overriding the use of those efforts and resources for our own benefit—without coming to see other people as threats and feeling hostility toward them. This point is dramatized in the account in *Atlas Shrugged* of the Starnes factory, which was reorganized by the founder's heirs on the principle "from each according to his ability, to each according to his need." Among the consequences of this policy was a loss of benevolence among the workers. "'Love of our brothers,'" says the tramp who tells the story to Dagny Taggart,

> 'that's when we learned to hate our brothers for the first time. We began to hate them for every meal they swallowed, for every small pleasure they enjoyed, for one man's new shirt, for another's wife's hat, for an outing with their family, for a paint job on their house — it was taken from us, it was paid for by our privations, our denials, our hunger.... In the old days we used to celebrate if somebody had a baby, we used to chip in and help him out with the hospital bills, if he happened to be hard-pressed for the moment. Now, if a baby was born, we didn't speak to the parents for weeks. Babies, to us, had become what locusts were to the farmers.'[9]

Accounts of life under communism provide real-world confirmation of Rand's analysis. When self-sacrifice for the common good was installed as the organizing principle of society, individuals became mean, petty, suspicious, hostile.[10] As Nathaniel Branden put it, "The choice is: altruism or good will, benevolence, kindness, love and human brotherhood."[11]

Thus it is clear that the Objectivist ethics rejects assumption (2) as well as assumption (1). What about the final claim in the conventional view of benevolence: that it is a major virtue? This claim cannot be supported on the basis of altruism, but we may still ask what status benevolence has in an egoistic ethics. Rand's view on this question is unclear. On the one hand, she did not include benevolence or any related concept on her list of cardinal virtues (the same list is contained in Galt's speech from *Atlas Shrugged* and in her essay "The Objectivist Ethics").[12] In "The Ethics of Emergencies" she argues that since emergencies like fires, shipwrecks, and floods are not the norm in human life, the help we provide to strangers in such situations is a minor issue in ethics, and the benevolent willingness to offer it is a minor virtue. In an interview with *Playboy* magazine, she apparently extended this point beyond emergencies, applying it to any sort of help we may give others: "My views on charity are very simple. I do not consider it a major virtue and, above all, I do not consider it a moral duty. There is nothing wrong with helping other people, if and when they are worthy of the help and you can afford to help them. I regard charity as a marginal issue."[13]

On the other hand, the concept of benevolence toward others is not restricted to emergencies; it has a much broader application to the varied forms of intercourse we have with others in the normal conditions of human existence. Rand never wrote about this broader context for benevolence in her philosophical essays, although her novels contain many incidents and exchanges among characters that suggest this virtue played a significant role in her moral outlook.

In any case, benevolence in the sense I am going to define it *is* an important virtue, and the importance I ascribe to it is consistent with, indeed required by, the other principles of the Objectivist ethics. Before we examine the reasons for this conclusion, however, we need to consider an argument on the other side, an implicit argument that I believe has led many Objectivists to consider benevolence a minor virtue at best. This argument turns on the relationship between benevolence as a character trait and the benevolent view of the universe—a relationship that is worth clarifying in its own right.

3 Benevolence and the "benevolent universe" premise

The virtues of benevolence are often seen as responses to failure, suffering, and loss on the part of others: kindness as distress over someone else's suffering, compassion as the ability to identify with another's sorrows, generosity as a willingness to give to or share with those in need. From an Objectivist standpoint, this view of benevolence as a response to the negative aspects of life would naturally lead one to regard it as a minor virtue.

In "The Ethics of Emergencies," as noted, Rand argued that disasters are not the norm; if they were, human life would be impossible. This is her basis for saying that providing help in emergencies is a marginal issue in ethics. But the issue here is broader. Failure, suffering, and loss occur in situations other than emergencies, and the denial that these are essential in human life is therefore a more sweeping statement than the one Rand makes regarding emergencies. The solace that Roark offers Mallory is presented in a positive light, as a virtuous action. But Mallory's condition was not a physical emergency. His suffering was caused by the disparity between his ideals and the world around him—a clash that in Rand's view is all too common. Emergencies by nature are rare and involve a gross departure from the normal course of events.

The same cannot be said about the death of a loved one, the loss of a job, the breakup of a relationship, or other events that may properly elicit our sympathy toward others. Nevertheless, Rand held that failure, suffering, and loss are not metaphysically *important* features of human life, whereas major virtues are concerned with features of life that are metaphysically important.

In *The Romantic Manifesto*, Rand explains her concept of metaphysical importance as follows:

> 'Important' — in its essential meaning, as distinguished from its more limited and superficial uses — is a *metaphysical* term. It pertains to that aspect of metaphysics which serves as a bridge between metaphysics and ethics: to a fundamental view of man's nature. That view involves the answers to such questions as whether the universe is knowable or not, whether man has the power of choice or not, whether he can achieve his goals in life or not. The answers to such questions are 'metaphysical value-judgments,' since they form the base of ethics.[14]

The issues that she mentions are not questions about what is possible in human life and in the world, but about what is normal. Of course some things may remain unknowable or unintelligible to a given person in a given context of knowledge; some people are constrained in their choices because they are victims of forces beyond their control; some people fail to achieve happiness despite their best efforts. The question is: what is the normal, the to-be-expected, and what is the exceptional, the accidental, the to-be-explained by special circumstances?

When I strike a match and it doesn't light, I look for a specific explanation: the match was wet, the wind was blowing too hard, etc. But when the match lights, no such explanation is called for; this is the normal, expected course of events. Failure and suffering are like the match's failing to light, success and happiness like the match's lighting. In saying that failure, loss and suffering are not metaphysically important, Rand meant that knowledge, success, happiness are the to-be-expected. Bewilderment, failure, and suffering are the not-to-be-expected; they should not form a part of one's conception of what life is like or about; when they occur they should be dealt with and if possible dispatched without dwelling on them.

This outlook, and its emotional expression, are conveyed in a passage from *Atlas Shrugged* describing Dagny's recovery from the enormously painful loss of her relationship with Francisco:

> She survived it. She was able to survive it, because she did not believe in suffering. She faced with astonished indignation the ugly fact of feeling pain, and refused to let it matter. Suffering was a senseless accident, it was not part of life as she saw it. She would not allow pain to become important. She had no name for the kind of resistance she offered, for the emotion from which the resistance came; but the words that stood as its equivalent in her mind were: It does not count—it is not to be taken seriously.[15]

This attitude is described as a benevolent sense of life, or the view of the universe as benevolent (something of a misnomer, since the universe does not literally have such attitudes as benevolence or malevolence). And the opposing viewpoint, the malevolent sense of life, has also been expressed artistically by writers like Thomas Hardy, Theodore Dreiser, and many others who wrote from a tragic sense of life.

If suffering and loss are *not* metaphysically important, if they are not the core of life, then the response to them cannot be the core of morality. Of course the possibility of these things *is* important for ethics. It is the conditional nature of life, the fact that living organisms must support their lives in the face of the constant alternative of death, that gives rise to values in the first place. Pain and suffering perform the vital function of alerting any sentient organism to conditions that are inimical to its life. And nothing guarantees the successful exercise of our capacities in the service of our lives. It is precisely the fallible, nonautomatic character of reason as the human means of survival that gives rise to the need for an explicit code of ethics. In this sense, all of the virtues in the Objectivist moral code are directed at achieving happiness and success in the face of possible suffering and failure.

Nevertheless, in a universe where achievement, success, and happiness are not only possible but normal, where they are the to-be-expected, the primary virtues must be those by which we pursue and achieve them: rationality, courage, productiveness, integrity, pride. The virtues required for coping with suffering and failure, when they do occur, are of secondary importance. We do not go out looking for suffering and loss to relieve, as we do look for occasions to exercise rationality, productiveness, and pride. Indeed, one of Rand's objections to altruism is that it gives its practitioners a vested interest in suffering and helplessness. In *The Fountainhead*, for example, Catherine Halsey discovers that as a social worker, her initial idealism has been replaced by a desire to see others remain dependent on her: "there was a girl who needed a job desperately — it was really a ghastly situation in her home, and I promised that I'd get her one. Before I could find it, she got a good job all by herself. I wasn't pleased. I was sore as hell that somebody got out of a bad hole without *my* help."[16]

Ironically, then, the benevolent view of the universe seems to imply that benevolence as a character trait is a minor virtue at best. The link between the metaphysical value judgment and the status of the virtue can be stated in terms of a deductive argument that summarizes the foregoing analysis:

1) Major virtues are concerned with metaphysically important features of human life

2) Failure, suffering, and loss are not metaphysically important in human life

3) The virtues of benevolence are concerned with failure, suffering, loss[17]

Therefore, the virtues of benevolence are not major virtues.

What is the rationale for the benevolent view of the universe? The fundamental issue that divides the benevolent from the malevolent view is whether man's capacities are adequate to meet his needs, within the environment in which he operates. Casting the issue in this biocentric form suggests a biocentric answer: a species whose capacities were not adequate to its needs, a species of whom the malevolent view was true, would be on its way to extinction, and this is manifestly not the case for humans. The deeper philosophical case for the benevolent view is provided by the Objectivist epistemology and metaphysics. The Objectivist epistemology establishes that reason is an open-ended source of objective knowledge about the world, answering such claims as that the senses are unreliable, that certainty is impossible, that reason is limited to the realm of appearances and cannot grasp things as they are in themselves. The Objectivist metaphysics, specifically its view of human nature, establishes that man's active powers are efficacious, giving him an open-ended power to create and achieve his values. This view of human nature includes the view of free will as the choice to think, the rejection of original sin, and the rejection of any inherent conflict between reason and emotion, mind and body, or thought and action. In short, the benevolent view of the universe is the product of a wide range of considerations drawn from the philosophy of Objectivism as a systematic whole.

It should be emphasized that this view is a philosophical thesis. It concerns the *fundamental* relationship between human nature and the reality in which we exist. It is the thesis that reality is auspicious to human life as such.[18] This thesis is perfectly consistent with the fact that many people live in *social* environments that are distinctly inimical to their survival. Terrorism, arbitrary rule, censorship, expropriation of wealth, and other forms of coercion interfere with the ability to act rationally and productively, and thus to achieve success. The benevolent view of the universe is based in part on the fact that man has free will, one consequence of which is that human beings may, through ignorance or viciousness, create destructive social environments. But the benevolent view denies that human beings are vicious or doomed to ignorance by nature. A free and civilized society is possible to man. Like any other value, however, it must be created through productive effort governed by reason. The benevolent universe thesis says that if human beings exert that effort they may expect success.

The thesis is also consistent with another fact often raised against it: the fact that prior to the 20th century most people lived in what we would now regard as conditions of abject poverty, and had few of the material comforts or prospects in life that we take for granted today. There is no denying that those of us living in contemporary industrialized countries are the beneficiaries of extraordinary technological and economic progress. And progress implies that life in the past was poorer in many respects than it is today. But while the level of production was lower 100 years, or 200 years, or 1,000 years ago, it was just as true then as now that man is capable of producing, and that reality is hospitable to a rational, productive mode of existence. That is what the benevolent view asserts. And the fact that progress is possible, that one generation can build on the productive achievements of previous generations, is itself a confirmation of the fit between man's powers and the world in which he exercises them.

It is worth noting, finally, that if the benevolent view of the universe seems to make benevolence a minor virtue at best, the converse is also true: those who see the universe in malevolent terms tend to elevate the virtues of benevolence into a central position. If life is a hopeless struggle, then the best we can hope for is some comfort along the way, and offering that comfort when we can is our primary obligation toward others. This is the essence of Bertrand Russell's argument in a famous essay:

> ...The life of man is a long march through the night, surrounded by invisible foes, tortured by weariness and pain, toward a goal that few can hope to reach, and where none may tarry long. One by one, as they march, our comrades vanish from our sight, seized by the silent orders of omnipotent death. Very brief is the time in which we can help them, in which their happiness or misery is decided. Be it ours to shed sunshine on their path, to lighten their sorrows by the balm of sympathy, to give them the pure joy of a never-tiring affection, to strengthen failing courage, to instill faith in hours of despair. Let us not weigh in grudging scales their merits and

demerits, but let us think only of their need—of the sorrows, the difficulties, perhaps the blindnesses, that make the misery of their lives; let us remember that they are fellow sufferers in the same darkness, actors in the same tragedy with ourselves.[19]

(Notice that Russell's view of life leads him to endorse not only sympathy and kindness, but also the other major element in Christian altruism: leniency in judgment, the "tempering" or replacement of justice by mercy.)

Before we conclude that benevolence is a minor virtue, however, we must question the other premise on which the conclusion rests: that benevolence is a response to failure, suffering, and loss. The association between benevolence and these negative aspects of life is not a necessary one, especially if we subscribe to the benevolent view of the universe. In the previous section, we saw that benevolence can be detached from its association with the altruist assumptions that are part of our cultural heritage. In the same way, it can be detached from the tragic sense of life that is also part of our heritage, largely because of the religious view of this world as a vale of tears and of this life as an ordeal in which we prepare for the life to come. In rejecting this view, as we reject altruism, we must reconceive the nature of benevolence. In what follows, I will show that the virtues of benevolence are directed primarily to the achievement of a positive value; and that the proper response to negative outcomes, when they do occur, is determined by the nature of that value.

In essence, I will argue, benevolence is a commitment to engage with others, to participate in society, in order to achieve the values derivable from other human beings. This commitment is based on the belief that one's interests are not in conflict with those of others, but in basic harmony. It involves the expectation that one will be able to like, respect, enjoy the company of, or at least profit economically from exchanges with, most of the people around one—that they will make a positive contribution to one's life. And it requires us to initiate certain actions, to deal with others in certain specific ways. As we will see, benevolence in this sense is not a product of a malevolent view of the universe, as in Russell's argument. It is an implication of the benevolent view as applied to society.

4 The analysis of virtues

Before examining benevolence itself, let us pause to consider the general requirements for analyzing a virtue. A virtue is a character trait, a standing commitment to a certain principle of action. Since human action is purposive, i.e., value-seeking, one essential element in a virtue is the value at which it aims. "*Value,*" as Rand says, "is that which one acts to gain and/or keep—*virtue* is the act by which one gains and/or keeps it."[20] The ultimate value we seek in all our actions is our own lives and happiness, but there are specific values we should seek to achieve, and specific policies of action, specific virtues, that are necessary for achieving them. Thus the virtue of rationality—the policy of using one's mind objectively to expand one's grasp of reality—is necessary to achieve the value of knowledge. Pride—the policy of seeking (and appreciating) one's own moral rectitude—is necessary to achieve the value of self-esteem. To understand benevolence, therefore, we must identify the values at which it aims.

We must also identify the facts on which it is based. In order to achieve our values, we have to take account of certain basic facts about the human condition. That is why we need virtues in the first place: we cannot achieve our ends by magic, whim, or random action; we must take account of facts about human nature, the world in which we act, and the causal relationships between actions and results. A virtue involves the recognition of such facts and the commitment to acting in accordance with them.[21] Thus pride is the recognition of the fact that "man is a being of self-made soul": we cannot achieve self-esteem without acting in such a way as to earn it. Rationality is the recognition of the most basic fact of all — that facts are facts, that A is A, and that reason is our only means of knowledge. Our second major task in understanding benevolence is therefore to identify the facts on which it is based.

It should be noted that the foregoing is a *philosophical*, not a *psychological* analysis of virtue. Psychologically, a virtue is normally experienced as a way of acting that seems obvious and automatic, not as the deliberate adoption of a policy in pursuit of a conscious goal. An honest man is normally truthful as a matter of course, without thinking consciously about the values he is seeking or the facts of reality that make honesty the best policy for achieving them. Nevertheless, a virtue must be a knowing commitment, not a blind habit or disposition of acting in a certain way.

For one thing, virtues cannot operate automatically all the time. There are situations in which the right course of action is not obvious; we must deliberate about how to apply our principles. This requires that we *have* principles regarding the fundamental values we seek and the facts of reality pertinent to them. Even when it operates automatically, moreover, a virtue must reflect an implicit awareness of these values and facts, held subconsciously as premises the person has accepted. If the habit is completely "blind," not based on any understanding, then it is not a virtue. For example, if a person's habit of telling the truth is supported only by fear of punishment and desire for his parents' approval, feelings which long survived his childhood because he never examined them, then he is not properly described as honest.

The philosophical analysis of a virtue, therefore, makes explicit what is normally an implicit rationale for the commitment to act in a certain way. The same analysis will allow us to determine whether a virtue is of major or minor importance. A virtue is a major one if and to the extent that the values at which it aims, and the facts on which it is based, are fundamental ones. Honesty, for example, is a commitment to maintain an unbreached cognitive contact with reality in all one's actions; to act on the basis of the truth, the whole truth, and nothing but the truth; and not to seek any value through deluding oneself or others. This commitment is based on the fact that cognition is man's primary means of pursuing any value, and that knowledge is the identification of what exists. These are fundamental facts about the human condition, and honesty is accordingly a major virtue. Cleanliness, by contrast, is based on the fact that dirt, sweat, and other grime can be hazardous to one's health as well as malodorous. Cleanliness is doubtless a virtue, but it is a minor one because these facts do not have the fundamentality of those on which honesty is based.

With this framework in hand, let us now consider the nature and status of benevolence.

5 The values at which benevolence aims

Benevolence is obviously concerned with our relationships with other people. The values we derive from these relationships are enormous: they touch every aspect of our lives. And they are diverse: they range from the products available at the local supermarket to the emotional rewards of intimacy. But these diverse values can be classified as instances of certain fundamental values.

Consider first the impersonal, more or less public relationships we have with others as members of society. At the broadest level of abstraction, Rand noted that the benefits made possible by man's social existence are communication and the exchange of goods and services.[22] The ability to communicate knowledge allows each of us to guide our actions by a much larger body of facts than would be possible if we were isolated knowers; to cooperate in pursuing our goals; and to build on the knowledge acquired by previous generations. The ability to exchange goods and services allows individuals to expand their own productive capacity through specialization, and to enjoy a vastly greater wealth of products than they could produce in isolation.

In addition to the utilitarian benefits of knowledge and wealth, we derive more personal values from certain people in our lives, such as companionship, emotional support, inspiration, friendship and romantic love. These benefits are instances of a fundamental value relating to the affirmation of one's identity as an individual. This value is less obvious and less widely understood than wealth and knowledge, but it is no less important. Each of us has an identity consisting in his goals, his principles and convictions, his character traits, his personality, his interests, his likes and dislikes. As a self-conscious being with a need for self-esteem, one needs to experience one's identity as something real and efficacious in the world. Other people can allow one to experience that identity in a way that is not possible by purely introspective means. In doing so, they provide the value of *visibility*, in two closely related forms:

1) Insofar as another person embodies something that I value as part of my own identity, he allows me to experience in concrete perceptible form, out there in the world, the traits which, in myself, I can experience only in an abstract and introspective form. A friend, as Aristotle said, is another self, and I see myself in him. If I love music, for example, the company of other music-lovers is enjoyable because it objectifies my interest. I see in others, in their visible excitement and eagerness to discuss the subject, the same feeling that I can otherwise experience only in the privacy of my own mind. This phenomenon extends beyond friends and companions. I may be inspired by the example of someone I have never met, someone with whom I can identify and whose achievement has a personal significance for me because it represents the success of my own values.

2) I also experience the affirmation of my identity from the process of interacting with another person. In the course of a conversation, for example, the other person is responding not merely to the physical sound of my speech but to the thoughts and feelings it expresses. Insofar as he understands and values those thoughts and feelings, his response allows me to experience their reality and value as objective. He makes me feel visible. In this respect, another person can be a psychological mirror, allowing me to see myself from the outside. Once again, he provides a concrete experience of those traits I value abstractly in myself.[23]

Economic exchange, communication, and mutual visibility, then, are the fundamental ways we derive benefits from others, in countless complex forms and combinations. But they are not ends in themselves. Economic exchange, communication, and visibility are the means — the instruments or processes — by which we acquire values from others. Those underlying values are wealth, knowledge, and self-affirmation, respectively. And our relationships with others are not the primary sources of these values. Exchange is not the fundamental source of wealth: production is. There can be nothing to trade until something is produced. The fundamental source of wealth is the creation of value by individuals pursuing a productive purpose. Similarly, communication is not the fundamental source of knowledge; reason is. There can be nothing to communicate until something has been discovered by individuals using reason to achieve a first-hand grasp of reality. Visibility, finally, is not the fundamental source of our identity or the value we place on it. As self-directed, self-made beings, we must achieve confidence in our values and a sense of identity — i.e., we must achieve self-esteem — through our own efforts. Other people cannot give us self-esteem; they can only reaffirm what we have already affirmed.

This is why reason, productive purpose, and self-esteem are the primary values in the Objectivist ethics, and rationality, productiveness, and pride are the cardinal virtues. They are the primary ways in which we relate to reality, including the reality of our selves. And this tells us that virtues concerned with our relationships with other people cannot be assigned the same degree of fundamentality.[24]

Nevertheless, the various forms of interaction with other people vastly multiply the scale of values we can acquire. To appreciate their power, one need only imagine the poverty, ignorance, and loneliness of life on the proverbial desert island. Imagine being limited in wealth to the things one can produce by one's own efforts, limited in knowledge to the things one can discover on one's own, and limited to one's own companionship and conversation. So the values derivable from others, while not at the ultimate level in the hierarchy of values, are at the penultimate level. They are next to cardinal in their importance.

The appropriate method of obtaining these values is through trade. "The principle of trade," Ayn Rand observed,

> is the only rational ethical principle for all human relationships, personal and social, private and public, spiritual and material. It is the principle of *justice*.
>
> A trader is a man who earns what he gets and does not give or take the undeserved. He does not treat men as masters or slaves, but as independent equals. He deals with men by means of a free, voluntary, unforced, uncoerced exchange....[25]

Rand is using the concept of trade in a broader sense than the exchange of economic goods and services. In this broader sense, communication and visibility are also forms of trade. They do not involve the literal transfer of a good; for example, in communicating what I know to someone else, I do not lose that knowledge myself, as I do give up money when I exchange it for a material good. Nevertheless, communication and visibility possess the two features essential to trade: each is i) a voluntary relationship in which ii) the parties derive mutual benefit.[26]

The trader principle endorses these two features of trade as a matter of justice. i) Insofar as a trade is a voluntary exchange, the trader principle involves a recognition of other people as rational beings who must have the freedom to act on their own judgment. ii) Insofar as a trade involves an exchange of value for value, the trader principle involves a commitment to judging the specific merits of what the other person is or has to offer. Such judgments obviously differ from one case to another. We spend our money on some goods but not on others. One person is qualified for a job, another is not. Some people have the traits of character that deserve our respect, others do not. In both respects, the trader principle is a commitment to recognizing people for what they are and dealing with them accordingly — and that is the essence of justice as a virtue. Even though justice is a virtue pertaining to our relationships with others, therefore, it is of fundamental importance and belongs on the list of major virtues.

But justice is not the only principle of action we need for dealing with people on the basis of trade. The principle of justice recognizes the necessity for identifying and evaluating people, for discriminating and making judgments, including moral judgments. The principle of justice says that when an opportunity for trade presents itself, we must judge it by its merits. But opportunities for trade do not simply present themselves. They must be created through our own initiative. The world does not beat a path to our door; we must go out to meet it; we must extend ourselves. In order to obtain the benefits of living with others in society, we cannot function solely as judges, we must also function as entrepreneurs.

For example, we value having friends, but how do we acquire them? By meeting people and getting to know them. We spend time with people, giving them our attention, taking an interest in who they are, what they do, what they like, what they believe and value. Most of the people with whom we do this will not become friends. In a large portion of the cases, we will not pursue any specific relationship at all. In such cases, the people will turn out not to have deserved our time, attention, effort. But there is no other way to find out than by investing these resources in the search. And most people will not be terribly eager to engage with us in this process unless we project at the outset an expectation of positive results, an invitation to trade. The principle of justice guides our search, giving us a standard for evaluating the results, but it is the principle of benevolence that commits us to the search in the first place. Justice disposes, but it is benevolence that proposes.

The function of benevolence in the pursuit of our rational self-interest, then, is to create opportunities for trade by treating other people as potential trading partners. The value at which it aims is trade — and the vast expansion of wealth, knowledge, and self-affirmation that trade makes possible.

6 The facts on which benevolence is based

The kinds of actions involved in pursuing these benefits will vary depending on the kind of trade involved — material, intellectual, or personal and emotional. They will vary depending on the other persons involved, the extent of our knowledge of them, the kind of relationship we already have, our judgment of the potential values to be gained, and numerous other facts. But there are certain basic facts about human beings as such that we must take account of in all our interactions with others. Benevolence as a general virtue, as a general policy for living in society with others who share a common nature and represent potential values, involves the recognition of these facts.

Humanity. If we expect to trade with other people, we must first of all recognize and treat them as people: as human beings who are conscious, who have inner lives and are capable of self-awareness. In virtue of this self-awareness, we all have a need for visibility, a harmony between what we know about ourselves from the inside and the way in which others treat us.

In its richest forms, visibility is provided by friends who have specific knowledge of us and respond to us in ways that express that knowledge. But as Branden noted, there is a kind of primitive visibility one can derive from playing with a pet — as in rough-housing with a dog, where the dog's actions convey its awareness that one's intent is playful, not hostile.[27] In between these extremes, there is a generalized form of visibility that human beings can provide each other even if they are strangers: the recognition of each other as human beings.

This visibility may take the form simply of the awareness of each other's presence. Think of how disconcerting it is to have another person be unaware of one's presence, as by not making room in an elevator, or by acting as if one is a piece of freight going in the same direction. Many of our interactions with others are partial; in many cases we would get what we want from a machine. Anyone who has worked behind a counter knows the difference between a customer who treats him as a vending machine and one who treats him as a human being.

A stranger cannot know anything about the personal significance of most of the events in one's life, and so cannot provide visibility in that regard. But there are "universal" events in human life — marriage, death, the birth of a child, etc. — whose general significance is common to us simply as human beings. When we recognize these events in the lives of strangers, offering congratulations on a marriage, or consolation for a death in the family, we are providing a kind of visibility.

The issue here is not just the recognition in our minds that we are dealing with human beings: that's a matter of simple rationality. The issue is conveying that awareness overtly through the whole array of gestures, greetings, pleasantries, congratulations, and consolations that make up the background hum of life in society. As participants in these exchanges, we recognize others and announce ourselves publicly as candidates for trade, even if no specific opportunity for trade is in the offing.

Independence. A closely related fact is that people possess free will, the power to choose and thus to act independently. The principle of trade is explicitly founded on this point; trade, as Rand said, is the only way for people to interact as "independent equals." The recognition of each other's independence — once again, not just the private awareness of that fact, but the overt, public expression of our awareness—is a precondition for trade. It is a way of acknowledging that trade requires the willing participation of the other person, pursuing his interest, not mine, through the exercise of his own judgment. No one likes to be bullied, pressured, condescended to, or treated as incompetent to make his own decisions, and people are generally—and reasonably—not eager to undertake trading relationships with those who treat them in these ways.

Individuality. Every human being has a unique identity, constituted by his specific beliefs, values, personality, style, and manner of functioning; by the specific abilities, knowledge, and virtues he has acquired; by his present circumstances, the history of his experience, his future aims and goals. These individual attributes determine whether and how we will able to interact with him productively; they are the assets that he brings to any trade.

Discovering these attributes requires sensitivity, an alertness to the psychological attributes and states of others, an element of benevolence that I will discuss presently. But the universal fact about human beings that is relevant to our understanding of benevolence in general is that they *are* unique individuals. And, being self-conscious, they naturally wish to be treated as such. This is why people so often resent being labelled, classified, "pigeonholed." The cognitive act of classification is a way of treating a group of units as identical, omitting their differences. This is of course a valid cognitive process, and some who resent its application to themselves may be trying to escape the responsibility of having any definite identity. But more often, in my experience, the attitude reflects an intense commitment to one's identity: a desire for recognition as a distinct person.

The overt recognition of another's individuality is an element in that "generalized respect and good will" which Rand says is appropriate among human beings. There is an old joke about a corporate executive at a retirement banquet in his honor. After his subordinates have sung his praises for everything he achieved during his career, he rises to thank them, saying, "I could not have

The facts on which benevolence is based

done any of this without you — or people very much like you." The observation might actually be true, but it is enormously deflating in the circumstances, hardly an expression of respect and good will.

Harmony of interests. As an exchange of values, trade benefits both parties, it serves both their interests. Every specific trade is an illustration of the general harmony of interests that makes it possible for humans to adopt the principle of trade as a general rule for their relationships with others. But the harmony of interests exists only to the extent that others accept the principle of trade as the rule for their own conduct. There is no harmony of interest between a trader and a thief, a predator, or anyone else who does not wish to live by trade. In this respect, benevolence is an expression of one's commitment to the trader principle. When I treat others benevolently, I convey to them that I do not see them as threats or as prey, whose success must come at my expense, but as potential allies from whom I seek opportunities for mutual gain.

We may now summarize the analysis of the values at which benevolence aims, and the facts on which it is based, in terms of a definition:

> *Benevolence is a commitment to achieving the values derivable from life with other people in society, by treating them as potential trading partners, recognizing their humanity, independence, and individuality, and the harmony between their interests and ours.*

Benevolence involves a kind of respect for others, not the respect we have for the particular virtues and achievements of someone we admire, but the generalized respect we should have for others as beings capable of virtue and achievement.[28] That capacity is grounds for respect, in light of the value it can create in our lives. And if we adhere to the benevolent view of the universe, the possibility that others will fail to exercise that capacity must be seen as metaphysically unimportant. Of course human viciousness does occur, just as failure, suffering, and loss do, and when it occurs it must be dealt with. But we have no reason to expect it without specific evidence, and it should not be the central focus of our relationships with others.

The role of such respect as a precondition for trade is captured in *Atlas Shrugged*, when Hank Rearden, having signed over the rights to Rearden Metal in response to blackmail by the government, feels such a lack of respect for the men around him that he no longer wishes to engage in trade with them. Walking home one night,

> He felt nothing at the thought of the looters who were now going to manufacture Rearden Metal. His desire to hold his right to it and proudly to be the only one to sell it, had been his form of respect for his fellow men, his belief that to trade with them was an act of honor. The belief, the respect and the desire were gone.... The human shapes moving past him in the streets of the city were physical objects without any meaning.[29]

7 Benevolence and productiveness

Benevolence so defined fills a kind of conceptual gap in the theoretical structure of the Objectivist ethics. In regard to nature, the realm of metaphysical facts,[30] Objectivism recognizes two kinds of mental action as virtues. One is the identification of what exists, the recognition of facts as facts, the commitment to understanding things as they are, objectively. This is the essence of rationality. The other is the imaginative projection of new ways to exploit the potential of what exists and thus to create things that will serve our purposes. This is the essence of productiveness. The principle of rationality is: "It is." The principle of productiveness is: "What if?"

To endorse the first without the second, rationality without productiveness, would be to foster a kind of contemplative and detached outlook on life — the outlook characteristic of Greek philosophy, which exalted man's reason but not his active powers. Aristotle, for example, held that contemplation was a purer exercise of reason than its use in making, doing, achieving things in the world. One of Rand's own great achievements was her unification of thought and action, theory and practice, by recognizing productiveness as a major virtue.

In regard to other people and their works, the realm of manmade facts, the Objectivist ethics recognizes the policy of identifying what exists, the commitment to understanding people as they are and evaluating them objectively. This is the virtue of justice. But Objectivism has not recognized the complementary virtue, akin to productiveness, of projecting ways to exploit the potential represented by other people, to create opportunities for trade, to remake our social environment in the image of our values. This is the role that I see for benevolence. And just as rationality without productiveness breeds a passive outlook on the world, so justice without benevolence breeds a kind of passive and cautious attitude toward interacting with others.

It might be argued that everything I have attributed to benevolence is already entailed by the principle of justice: the latter asserts that we should recognize people for what they are and treat them accordingly; since other people are potential trading partners, it is a requirement of justice to act in such a way as to discover and create opportunities for trade. This is true, as far as it goes. It is also true that productiveness is entailed by the principle of rationality. Rationality is the commitment to identifying facts and acting accordingly. Since it is a fact that man's life must be supported by production, rationality requires that we act to create value by remaking the world. As my colleague Roger Donway once put it, nature, to be obeyed, must be commanded. Indeed, all of the virtues in the Objectivist ethics can be regarded as forms of rationality, insofar as they involve the recognition of certain facts as guides to action.

But the principle "Live by reason" is insufficiently specific to serve as a moral code all by itself. Concepts for other virtues serve to identify what it is that reason requires in regard to the fundamental and pervasive features of human life. The analysis I have offered, and the analogy between productiveness and benevolence, shows why benevolence should be regarded as a major virtue and why it should be distinguished from justice. Justice is a form of the "It is" principle. Its focus is on the actual. Benevolence is a "What if?" virtue whose focus is the potential of others.

Justice and benevolence have often been seen as conflicting virtues. The Christian tradition insists that justice be "tempered" by mercy. The dictionary includes "leniency in judgment" as part of the meaning of the word "charity." And Rand has her villain Ellsworth Toohey express the view that kindness is more important than justice.[31] But on the analysis offered here, there is no possibility of conflict. Benevolence is a commitment to achieving certain values in our relationships with others. If it becomes clear that those values are not available from a specific person—for example, if his behavior or character make him a positive threat—then it is not an act of benevolence to extend sympathy, kindness, or generosity.

The analogy with productiveness is illuminating in this respect. Productiveness is not mere industriousness, the willingness to put forth effort. Production is the exercise of reason for the purpose of creating value; those who act in violation of reason are accordingly not being productive. A person who doggedly tries to invent a perpetual motion machine is not acting from a surfeit of productiveness, but from a deficit of rationality; he is trying to get something for nothing, in disregard of the law of causality. In the same way, extending sympathy to terrorists is an act of injustice, not benevolence: it is hardly benevolent to support those who destroy human life. Giving money to those who beg by choice, when they could work for a living, is likewise an act of injustice rather than benevolence: it is not benevolent to encourage vice in others. In short, the values at which benevolence aims, and the facts on which it is based, must be used to determine which actions are truly benevolent in a specific context. And since these values and facts are consistent with those on which justice is based, there is no conflict between the virtues.

It is important, finally, to distinguish the *virtue* of benevolence from the *emotion*. The degree of warmth we feel toward others, the degree of interest we take and concern we have for them, is highly variable. It varies from one person to another as a matter of personality: some people are outgoing by nature, others are reserved. Such feelings also vary from day to day, from one situation to the next, for any given person. Nevertheless, the virtue of benevolence is a commitment to a policy of action, not of feeling. Just as it is possible to be rational while feeling confused, courageous while feeling frightened, or productive while feeling tired, it is possible to be benevolent while feeling absorbed in one's own cares.

Suppose I have just lost my job. It was a sudden thing—I did not expect to be laid off—and I cannot think of anything but my own plight. How will I go about finding work? How long can my family go without my earnings? As I think about these questions on the train home, feeling anxious about the future and sad at the loss of a job I liked, I see the people around me talking, reading, acting as they normally do, and their very normalcy is alienating. I do not feel benevolently toward them. I have no wish to strike up a conversation. But I am still capable of recognizing that the people around me are human; that they did not cause my problems and their enjoyment of life does not make my life worse; and that I should treat them with civility rather than rudeness or malice. This is all the virtue of benevolence requires in this context. Just as the virtue of productiveness does not require that one devote every waking hour to work, benevolence does not require that one take every opportunity to engage with others.

To be sure, we would not experience a person's benevolence as genuine if it were completely divorced from any feeling—if his action were entirely a product of an intellectual commitment to certain principles without any felt concern for us as beneficiaries. In the same way, we would justifiably wonder about the productiveness of a person who reported to work every day but never showed any interest in his job. These doubts arise because emotions reflect the premises one accepts. A person who fully accepts the principle on which a virtue is based will naturally come to feel the corresponding emotions: he will take pleasure in exercising his reason, in supporting his life through productive work, in treating others benevolently. An evident lack of such feelings is a symptom of an inner conflict, a less-than-full acceptance of the principle. But it is still the principle, not the feeling per se, that constitutes the virtue.

There is a final analogy with productiveness that should be mentioned, indeed stressed. The fundamental requirement of productiveness is to support oneself in some form of productive achievement. But productiveness obviously does not cease to be an issue once one has found a job. It is an ongoing commitment to create value in the world, to build, to grow, to expand one's skills and the scale of one's endeavors. In the same way, benevolence does not cease to be an issue once one has formed a trading relationship; it is an ongoing commitment to realize the potential of that relationship. I have focused on benevolence among strangers because there we are dealing with a pure potential, and the need for benevolence is clearest. But every actual relationship is at the same time a potential future one, dependent on the choice of the other person, and the preconditions for trade must therefore be maintained over time. It is with the people we already value that benevolence is most important—and can be most difficult. It is an exercise of benevolence to remember that an employee is an independent human being who should be treated with respect. It is an exercise of benevolence to give one's spouse the benefit of the doubt in the midst of an emotional conflict, attributing the better motive rather than the worse. And virtually any relationship has potential beyond the values that we have already derived from it, a potential to which we ought to remain alert.

Benevolence is a very general trait. That generality is inherent in the role it plays as a major virtue in the Objectivist ethics. But let us now consider some of its specific forms: the kinds of actions, habits, and policies that are part of the practice of benevolence. In what follows, I will discuss three of the specific virtues of benevolence: civility, sensitivity, and generosity. This is not intended as an exhaustive list, but I believe these three virtues are the most important components of benevolence. And they illustrate the ways in which the general principles we have discussed are applied to specific aspects of life with others in society.

8 Civility

Civility or common courtesy is the most elementary form of benevolence. It is an expression of respect toward others as beings who possess the basic human attributes in virtue of which they are potential values. Of the attributes we discussed above, civility is specially concerned with the humanity and independence of others, and with the harmony of interests. Saying *hello* and *good-bye, how are you?* and *have a nice day,* are ways of acknowledging that even if we know nothing else of a person, we know that he is human and that things can go well or poorly for him. Saying *please* and *thank you* is a way of acknowledging that another person is not our servant, pet, or infant, but an independent adult who is dealing with us by choice. Holding a door for another person, waiting our turn in line, and various other actions are ways to smooth over the minor collisions of life and thus preserve the harmony of interests. A person who is told to "keep a civil tongue" is being instructed not to escalate a dispute into a conflict; in this respect, civility is a disposition to look for peaceful and productive resolutions of disputes.

As the most elementary of the virtues of benevolence, civility is the most universal. It is appropriate even to strangers, appropriate especially to strangers, with whom we have no other relationship to guide us in our encounters. For that same reason, civility

typically involves the use of conventions that are widely understood within a society. The word "civility" and its equivalents, "po-
liteness" and "courtesy," derive from words designating the city
(*civis, polis*) or the court—historically the most advanced forms of
civilized life. As the etymology suggests, the standards of civility
serve to facilitate social intercourse of the complex kind associated
with complex social orders, and these standards inevitably have
an element of convention.

Every civilized society has various conventions regulating
common kinds of interactions among people: meeting in the street,
addressing a person by name or title, sharing a meal, courting a
member of the opposite sex, visiting someone else's home, giving
presents, taking part in ceremonies like marriage. This is the realm
of manners, involving standards for what is polite, appropriate,
correct, decent, seemly, decorous. Civility pertains only to a portion of this domain, that concerned with *common* courtesy: those
forms of behavior that express general respect for others and help
avoid conflicts. But these forms of civility do typically involve a
conventional element. There is no way to prove—as a universal
ethical proposition, derived from the standard of man's life as a
rational animal—that one should utter the word "please" in ask-
ing for the salt.

The forms of civility, and the broader realm of manners, are
therefore dismissed by some people as arbitrary. "Why should I
conform to arbitrary social standards? I am an individualist." But
while the forms are conventional, what is conveyed through those
forms is not. If my argument so far has been correct, then it *is* objectively important to acknowledge each other's independence in some
way or other, whether by saying "please," or "s'il vous plait," or
by some gesture understood to have that meaning. It doesn't matter which forms we use to convey this, any more than it matters
which sounds we use to express a given concept in language. But
insofar as civility has a communicative function, it does matter that
we use the same forms. Someone who does not practice these forms
is rude. We can assume that his failure to comply reflects indiffer-

ence to what the forms express (unless he is ignorant, as in the case of a foreigner).

A similar answer can be given to the complaint that the forms of civility are inauthentic. "What if I don't like the present Grandma gave me and I don't really feel any gratitude? Am I not falsifying my feeling if I say *thank-you* nonetheless?" The purpose of the thank-you is not to convey one's specific feelings about the gift, or the person who gives it. Its purpose is to acknowledge that it was a gift, from an autonomous person, not something owed one by an underling. (If Grandma wants more than this, and makes it clear that she really wants to know whether one liked the gift, then one should tell her, as tactfully as possible.)

Civility, then, may be defined as *the expression – chiefly through conventional forms – of one's respect for the humanity and independence of others, and of one's intent to resolve conflicts peacefully.*

9 Sensitivity

Trade in all its forms — material exchange, communication, and visibility — is an inherently social action. It therefore requires awareness of those with whom we trade, a kind of entrepreneurial alertness to opportunity. The opportunities for trade are created primarily by the psychological features of others: their interests, ideas, values, feelings, concerns, and worries. Sensitivity is the name for the policy of attending to, being alert to, these traits.

Among friends, of course, such awareness is necessary to maintain the friendship. It is part of the value we gain from friends and confer upon them. Sensitivity is the correlate of visibility: I am made to feel visible by my friend's sensitivity to me. But it is appropriate toward strangers as well, as a source of information about them as well as a way of expressing interest in them as potential trading partners. At the minimal level, some degree of sensitivity is a precondition for civility. Much rudeness is thoughtlessness: a failure to notice how some action unnecessarily offends, annoys, or causes pain to another. (An old definition of a gentleman is: one who never insults another person unintentionally.)

One of the less frequently noticed aspects of Rand's novels is the sensitivity of her characters. In *The Fountainhead*, as Neera Kapur Badhwar has observed,[32] there are a number of occasions on which Roark or Dominique try to control their reactions to another person in order to spare him the pain of showing what he has revealed. For example, when Roark sees Keating for the first time after many years, "Roark knew that he must not show the shock of his first glance at Peter Keating—and that it was too late: he saw a faint smile on Keating's lips, terrible in its resigned acknowledgment of disintegration."[33]

The scene in which Roark first visits Mallory, the scene to which I referred at the beginning of this essay, illustrates the kindness of which Roark is capable because of his sensitivity to Mallory's unspoken feelings. That sensitivity is illustrated in pure form after Mallory has recovered: "'Now,' [Roark] said, 'talk. Talk about the things you really want said. Don't tell me about your family, your childhood, your friends or your feelings. Tell me about the things you *think*.' Mallory looked at him incredulously and whispered: 'How did you know that?'"[34]

In *Atlas Shrugged*, Dagny is leaving her private car on the Taggart Comet when she hears an altercation between the conductor and a tramp outside her car; the conductor is ordering the tramp off the train. Dagny notices that despite the tramp's old and patched clothing, his shirt collar was laundered; and that even as he prepared to jump off the moving train, probably to his death, he tightened his grip on his bag. "It was the laundered collar and this gesture for the last of his possessions—the gesture of a sense of property—that made her feel an emotion like a sudden, burning twist within her."[35]

These are among the many examples in Rand's novels of the unusually perceptive degree of sensitivity she attributes to her characters. They can be taken as examples of compassion, kindness and/or sympathy as well as sensitivity, and the case for regarding sensitivity as the key virtue can be clarified by examining the relationships among these concepts.

The words "sympathy" and "compassion" derive, respectively, from Greek and Latin roots meaning "to feel with." They refer to the human ability to "enter into" another's mental state and feelings, to take on those feelings imaginatively as if they were one's own, and to feel some affinity with that person as a result. "Compassion" is the narrower term, being directed specifically to the suffering or sorrow of another person. "Sympathy" is broader, "signifying a general kinship with another's feelings, no matter of what kind."[36] One can sympathize with another's perplexity at a strange turn of events, his love for mountain landscapes, his feeling of triumph at solving a difficult problem.

Kindness is closely related to sympathy, but involves a more active desire to support the other person in whatever it is that he is experiencing. Where the experience is one of failure, suffering or loss, kindness involves the extension of psychological aid and comfort. It is opposed to cruelty: the indifference to — or worse, the active enjoyment of — another's pain. But kindness, like sympathy, is not merely a response to negative conditions. It is kind to remember someone's birthday, or to join in the celebration of another's achievement, or not to intrude on the privacy of a couple who wish to be alone.

Which of these concepts best captures the specific virtue of benevolence we are discussing? My argument throughout has been that the virtues of benevolence are not directed solely or primarily toward the negative. Compassion is therefore too narrow a concept. The remaining ideas — sensitivity, sympathy, and kindness — can be arranged on a continuum. Sensitivity is a purely cognitive phenomenon, the sheer awareness of another person's condition. At the other extreme, kindness involves a desire to act on the person's behalf, based on one's awareness of his condition. This desire may or may not be appropriate, depending on whether and to what extent the person was responsible for his own plight; and whether and to what extent he acknowledges any such responsibility.

Sympathy falls between sensitivity and kindness. The ability to identify with another's state goes beyond mere awareness, even if it does not involve an impulse to act on his behalf. To feel with another is to accept that feeling as one's own in an imaginative way, as something one would feel in the same situation; and to accept it as legitimate, as something it is appropriate to feel. Sensitivity per se may not give rise to either of these consequences. I may be sensitive to someone's fear of open spaces, even though that fear is so foreign to me that I cannot really imagine it as my own. And it would be positively unjust, as we noted, to sympathize with a vicious feeling like a terrorist's exultation in the death of his victim.

Sensitivity is the alertness to the psychological condition of others. It is the concept that best captures the virtue in question here because it is the more general virtue. The willingness to treat others with sympathy and kindness, although certainly components of benevolence, are narrower in scope because they are subject to additional conditions.

10 Generosity

Generosity is the final element of benevolence to be discussed. By contrast with sensitivity, kindness, and sympathy, it is concerned with the existential aid we provide to others. This act of helping others is the aspect of benevolence that people most often associate with altruism, and it is the issue about which egoists are most often questioned.

The essence of a generous act is providing another person with a good that is not part of a definite trade, giving something without the expectation of a definite return. The good need not be material. It could be one's time or talent. It could even be one's judgment of the person, giving him the benefit of the doubt, placing a generous construction on acts that are not conclusively vicious. The question is: what rationale can be offered for a generous act by an egoistic ethic in which trade is the proper relationship among people? Let us consider three common motives for generosity, each of them selfish in a different way.

1) Sometimes we act generously as an expression of our own happiness. I feel exuberantly happy, and I want others to share in my condition; it makes my happiness more real. I have just gotten a huge raise and I want to take everyone I work with out to dinner. Generosity in this sense is a kind of magnanimity: a spirit of overflowing with one's own efficacy, joy, success. It is related to

Aristotle's concept of liberality in giving, as an expression of pride in one's efficacy. Rearden gave presents to his family partly from this sense of pride.[37] This sort of generosity is certainly agreeable, but there is no apparent reason for regarding it as a virtue per se, as something morally required. There are many possible expressions of happiness and success, of which this is only one, and there is no apparent moral reason for distinguishing among them. It seems a matter of personality.

2) Another motive pertains to the sort of situation that Rand described in her essay: an emergency where someone is in trouble and we can help at little cost to ourselves. This *is* a moral issue, but the selfish rationale for extending help in such situations has not been fully analyzed by Rand or other Objectivists. The standard argument is that we give help because of the potential value that the other person represents. He might become a friend, or a partner in an economic exchange. Even if we never again have face-to-face dealings with him, it may still be true that as a productive person in an integrated economy, he will make a marginal contribution to our well-being. This is true, but the expected benefit can be so minute as to be negligible, not enough to justify any use of our own resources or the assumption of any measurable risk. And in any case, there is another issue involved.

Humans live together partly because there is safety in numbers. Throughout much of their existence as a species, human beings have lived in small bands of hunters and gatherers. The solidarity of the tribe was the only protection each individual had against the risks of starvation, predators, and attack by other tribes. The reciprocity within the tribe was relatively undefined and undelimited; it was one-for-all and all-for-one. By and large, the progress of civilization has been marked by the substitution of contract for the informal, indefinite, tradition-bound forms of reciprocity that characterize primitive tribes. We do not pool the harvest and share it among us; we buy our food in the market. Even emergencies are largely handled through contract and the division of labor. We hire firefighters, police, Coast Guard sailors, and other specialists. But there is a residual category of cases in which we can help each other avoid harm and risk, or gain benefits, in ways that are not easily reduced to contract, such as calling the police when we see a crime, calling the ambulance when we see an accident, sending food to areas hit by hurricanes or earthquakes, etc.

It is to the benefit of each of us to live in a society where people extend help in such cases. If I am a victim, it is certainly to my benefit to receive help; my life may depend on it. But there cannot be a society in which such help is available unless people extend help when they can. Not to do so is therefore to be a free-rider. Someone who would accept help in an emergency but would not provide it to others is acting on the premise of seeking something for nothing. He is seeking a benefit without the effort of producing that benefit; he wants to obtain an end without pursuing the necessary means. His action is therefore incompatible with independence and responsibility, which require that we make our own actions the causes of the benefits we enjoy, rather than depending on others to provide those benefits for us.

There are many technical questions surrounding the issue of free-riders; the preceding is intended only as a general statement of the essential Objectivist approach to the issue. But one complication deserves mention here. The rationality of extending aid is dependent on one's social environment. If one lives in a society where bad political institutions or cultural premises have created widespread suspicion, hostility, and conflict among people, and where people therefore do not generally help each other, then the argument above may not apply. It may no longer be in one's interest to provide help to strangers; it may even be dangerous. This is yet another illustration of the difference between egoistic and altruistic views of benevolence. The latter would require, or at least regard as noble, the self-sacrificial exercise of generosity even in socially malevolent situations.

As a form of generosity, then, giving aid to others in emergencies is self-interested not only because of the potential value to us of the person we help, but also because of the value to ourselves of a society in which such aid is available when we need it for ourselves and those we care for. And this points to another gap in the standard Objectivist view of such cases. Leonard Peikoff writes, "Extending help to others in such a context is an act of generosity, not an obligation."[38] It is certainly not an obligation in the strong sense that the recipient has a *right* to it. The donor must be free to assess the values and risks in the context of his own situation and hierarchy of values. But if an act of help is objectively appropriate, then it is morally required and the failure to provide that help is morally culpable. To take a famous example from the 1960s: when Kitty Genovese was stabbed to death outside her New York apartment, the people who heard her screams without calling the police did something *wrong*.

3) A third motive for generosity involves a kind of investment. One gives something to a person, not because he deserves it now, or because it is part of any definite trade, but because one senses that some long-range good may come of it. An investment in the literal financial sense, of course, is a trade, not an act of generosity. One exchanges a sum of money for a right to a share in specific future benefits subject to specific conditions. The form of generosity in question here is thus an investment only in an extended or metaphorical sense. My whole argument has been that benevolence in general is a kind of investment in this sense: one invests one's time, attention, and concern in people in order to create opportunities for trade, even though many of them won't pan out. But there are much more specific forms of generosity as investment.

An example from *Atlas Shrugged* is Dagny's invitation to the tramp to have dinner, after she has saved him from being thrown off the train.[39] We have already discussed her alertness to the marks of his self-respect as an example of sensitivity. The dinner invitation was an act of generosity. It certainly was not required as an act of justice. But in the world of *Atlas Shrugged*, where competence, self-respect, and civility were fast disappearing, she was eager to see any sign of these qualities, and probably felt she could make use of them somehow. (As it turns out, her investment paid off handsomely: she learns from the bum about the Starnes factory, the last in a series of stories told about the "mythical" John Galt, this one the truth.)

Hank Rearden's indulgent attitude toward the Wet Nurse is another example of generosity as investment. The Wet Nurse is a government flunky sent to regulate the sale of Rearden Metal. In function he is a parasite, part of the oppressive government regulations that effectively expropriate Rearden's ownership of his own achievement. In character, the Wet Nurse is an utter pragmatist, with "no inkling of any concept of morality."[40] Rearden owes him nothing, and in justice could certainly have condemned him as a vicious enemy. Yet the boy's sneaking admiration for Rearden suggests to him that there might be a virtuous streak behind the cynical mask, and Rearden's attitude is one of amused indulgence rather than resentment. Here too the investment pays off, when the Wet Nurse comes to understand the moral principles at stake and tries to defend Rearden's mills against attack.

This sort of investment in people is a clear illustration of the difference between justice and benevolence, between the "It is" and the "What if?" One often meets someone of undistinguished character, ability or attainment in whom one senses the potential for something better. In considering what he deserves as a matter of justice, we must base our judgment on his actual traits and achievements, not on some potential which he has chosen never to exercise. But a benevolent person goes on to ask: What if he did make that choice? Is there some way it can be encouraged? And very often it is the act of investing that provides the encouragement. The fact that someone is willing to "take a chance" on him—to give him a job or a loan, say, or to meet with him socially—creates a desire not to disappoint the benefactor. It may give that person the courage and confidence he needs to do what he has never done before. It may give him the sense that the world is open to his efforts.

What is the selfish reason for making such an investment? It may be the expectation that in some way, at some time, the person one is helping will do something that repays one's efforts. But it may be a more general sense that one's own life is improved by living in a world with better, happier, more fully realized people in it. This is a way of creating value in the world, by analogy with productive work. Here again, the parallel between benevolence and productiveness is illuminating. A truly productive person is motivated not only by the monetary return for his work but also by the satisfaction of creating value. The creation of value is the primary motive for work; the money one earns is a social recognition of that value but cannot replace one's own judgment and commitment as its source. In the same way, there is a satisfaction in creating value in the lives of others, a satisfaction that remains even when the value cannot be returned in the form of a definite trade. This parallel between benevolence and productiveness is captured in *The Fountainhead*, where Roark, now working for Peter Keating's firm, helps the latter with his designs: "Roark looked at the sketches, and even though he wanted to throw them at Keating's face and resign, one thought stopped him: the thought that it was a building and that he had to save it, as others could not pass a drowning man without leaping in to the rescue."[41]

The foregoing examples involved investments made in the context of a personal relationship. There are also social institutions that mediate impersonal investments. A great deal of work in education, research, and art (as well as the provision of aid to victims of emergencies) is conducted by nonprofit organizations funded through voluntary contributions. Those who donate to these organizations are helping to create value without a specific contractual relationship or a return that is specific to their effort; those who donate less, or nothing at all, still gain the benefits created by the organization's work. Donors are therefore acting from a spirit of generosity.

Their generosity may reflect the desire not to be a free-rider. To the extent that one benefits from the existence of such organizations, it is rational to support them. In many rural areas of the United States, for example, fire departments and rescue squads are staffed by volunteers and supported by donations. People who live in those areas benefit directly and should give accordingly. In many other cases, however, it is more natural to regard charitable contributions as more general investments in the value created by colleges and universities, museums, medical research centers, political advocacy groups, and the like.

Such generosity is not altruistic. As an investor, one should not give in response to need per se, but in response to the promise and potential for creating value. One should not give aid merely because a person needs it, but because he can better his life with it. One does not give money to philanthropic organizations merely because they're short on cash, but because they are capable of using the money productively.[42] And each of us should give in accordance with his own hierarchy of values. One could easily give away his entire income to worthy causes, including the relief of suffering. The kind of altruism which says we must apportion our time between what we do for ourselves and what we do for others (see page 7 above) offers no principled guidance on how to draw the line. If the needs of others create claims on our time and resources, why do we honor some of these claims but not others? On the Objectivist view, by contrast, helping others is a self-interested action, and the choice of how much to help is an economic decision like any other. It is no different in principle from the decision of how to choose between more work and more leisure, how much to save for retirement, how much insurance to buy, whether to read a book or weed the garden. All of these questions must be resolved by reference to one's *own* hierarchy of values.

Generosity is a complex element in the general virtue of benevolence. Of the three types of generosity we have discussed — celebration, aid in emergencies, and investment in potential — only the latter two are relevant to generosity as a moral virtue. That virtue may be defined accordingly as *the willingness to provide others with goods without the expectation of a definite return, either as aid in an emergency or as a nonspecific investment in their potential.*

11 Conclusion

We can draw together the conclusions of this essay in terms of two complementary questions. The first is: Why does it matter for Objectivists to recognize benevolence as a major virtue? It matters because of the importance to us of the values we gain from others: economic exchange, the communication of knowledge, and the reaffirmation of our own identity. These are all forms of trade among individuals, and to live by trade requires benevolence as well as justice. Benevolence is a creative virtue, a kind of productiveness applied to our relationships with others. It is a commitment to achieving the values derivable from living together with others by treating them as potential trading partners, through the exercise of such component virtues as civility, sensitivity, and generosity.

The second and complementary question is: Why does it matter for our understanding of benevolence to give it an Objectivist foundation? It is important to make clear, first of all, that benevolence is not altruism. It does not involve any sacrifice on our part, nor any acceptance of sheer need, sheer lack (the zero, as Rand put it) as a claim on wealth or ability. My analysis has shown the diverse ways in which benevolence serves one's rational, long-term interests. This analysis also shows that the virtues of benevolence are not essentially responses to failure, suffering and loss; they con-

51

sist in a positive commitment to creating opportunities for trade. Finally, the Objectivist approach removes the tension between benevolence and justice by showing how they are complementary and consistent virtues.

Objectivism has often been described as a philosophy of "rugged individualism." The rugged individualist is the frontiersman keeping his distance from organized society, heading over the next mountain range when he sees the chimney smoke of settlers coming near. He is the sharp-elbowed trader who sees the essence of life as competition and conflict. My analysis of benevolence as a virtue makes it clear that these are false images of individualism. The *rational* individualist is not the enemy of benevolence or civility, but their truest exemplar.

Appendix Tolerance

Although I have mentioned tolerance as an element of benevolence, I did not include it as a component virtue on a par with civility, sensitivity, and generosity. This deserves a word of explanation, especially since I have discussed tolerance at length in another work, *Truth and Toleration*.[43]

I noted there that the concept of tolerance applies in many realms, but that its core meaning in all applications is "to endure, allow, or put up with something." This core meaning involves two essential elements: a) The object of tolerance—that which we tolerate—must be something with a negative value significance, something wrong, false, dangerous, painful, etc. b) To tolerate this object is to forbear from taking some action against it, to forbear from opposing, removing, or condemning it. Where these conditions do not obtain, the concept is not applicable. In particular, if something has a positive value significance, then there is nothing to tolerate. We do not endure or put up with the good, the true, the beautiful; we actively embrace them. Even if something is of neutral significance, neither good for us nor bad, there is nothing to tolerate; there is no action of opposing, removing, or condemning it from which we need to forbear.

Truth and Toleration dealt with tolerance in the realm of ideas, as a policy toward those with whom one disagrees, those whose

53

ideas one believes to be false. The policy is not to condemn or ostracize a person morally because of his beliefs. The fact that someone's belief is false does not entail that he is irrational in holding it, since there are many sources of innocent error, especially in regard to political, philosophical, and other complex issues. Thus we cannot judge the person morally without knowing more about how he came to believe what he does; we cannot infer that he is immoral merely from the false content of his beliefs. Note that the object of tolerance is not the beliefs—we should criticize and oppose them if we are convinced they are false—but the person who holds these beliefs.

This negative aspect of toleration is a matter of simple justice: it is unjust to condemn a person morally on insufficient evidence. But there is a positive rationale for tolerance as well. Its primary function as a virtue, I argued, "is to provide a necessary condition for open discussion and debate among rational people."[44] Intellectual exchange with those who disagree with us is an invaluable means of testing, clarifying, enriching, and deepening our own view of reality. Our opponents can alert us to considerations we might have overlooked, or dismissed too quickly. They can serve as useful predators, picking off our weaker arguments. The willingness to engage in discussion and debate is not a mark of scepticism or relativism, but an effective means of achieving certainty:

> A conclusion is certain if it is proven beyond a reasonable doubt; the conclusion must integrate all the available evidence, and the available evidence must rule out the possibility of any other conclusion. Because certainty is a relation between an individual mind and reality, it does not depend epistemologically on any commerce with one's fellows. For all the reasons I have stated, however, such commerce is a psychological necessity—at least in regard to the sorts of complex issues we're concerned with. To know that a conclusion integrates all the available evidence, one must know that he has made all the relevant evidence available to himself, and drawn out its implications properly. To know that no other conclusion is consistent with the evidence, he must know that he has considered the relevant alternatives. Our assurance on this score

rests partly on the knowledge that we have been open to the insights of our opponents, and fairly met their objections.[45]

For all these reasons, which are discussed at greater length in *Truth and Toleration,* tolerance is an important *intellectual* virtue. But it pertains specifically to the realm of *ideas,* to matters of conviction and controversy, which constitute only one department of our relationships with others.[46] Tolerance in this sense lacks the generality of civility, sensitivity, and generosity, which apply to all the values we gain through trade. The question, then, is whether there is a broader concept of tolerance that applies to all these values. In contemporary moral discourse, the concept is indeed used more broadly. But I believe that "tolerance" in this broader sense is not a valid concept. It represents an internally inconsistent attempt to integrate things that are fundamentally dissimilar.

Tolerance is widely advocated as an antidote to prejudice and bigotry. We are urged to tolerate those who differ from us in race, sex, ethnicity, sexual orientation, and other characteristics rather than allowing those differences to breed contempt and hostility among groups. And there is no denying that such hostility is a pervasive social problem. In the United States today, for example, mutual suspicion and resentment between whites and blacks has reached toxic proportions. Throughout the world, ethnic animosity has produced hatred of immigrants, discriminatory legislation, and bloodshed. The concept of tolerance, however, is a pitifully superficial response to this problem.

The problem is one of irrationality, and specifically of what Ayn Rand called the anti-conceptual mentality: the syndrome which "treats abstractions as if they were *perceptual* concretes."[47] The anti-conceptual mentality regards a concept as a self-contained given, as something that requires no logical process of integration and definition. This syndrome is motivated by the desire to retain the effortless, automatic, and infallible character of perceptual awareness, and to avoid the mental independence, effort, and risk of error that conceptual integration entails. In the anti-conceptual mentality, "the process of integration is largely replaced by a process of association."[48] People who function this way are typically unable to define their terms; for them, the meaning of a word is a jumble of memorized examples, emotional connotations, and floating images. And their convictions tend to be held as slogans, detached from logic and evidence; they are unable to think in principles.

In numerous ways, as Ayn Rand observed, the anti-conceptual mentality breeds an identification with and dependence upon the group, usually a group united by such concrete traits as race, sex, or geographical proximity. The moral universe of such people is constituted by concrete substitutes for ethical principles: customs, traditions, myths, rituals, and the like. Those who belong to different tribes, with different concretes, are naturally regarded with suspicion at best. The anti-conceptual mentality is incapable of abstracting from concrete differences among people and formulating general principles of common human rights, or common standards for judging an individual's moral character and conduct. Its sense of right and wrong is anchored not in reality but in loyalty to the tribe and its practices; the solidarity of the tribe is sustained in part by hostility toward outsiders.

The proper antidote to bigotry, then, is rationality, including the commitment to a fully conceptual mode of functioning. How else could one come to understand the injustice of discriminating among people on the basis of morally irrelevant characteristics? How else could one understand trade as the proper principle for human relationships, and benevolence as a precondition for trade?

Christianity, among other major world religions, has attempted to counter bigotry through the spirit of universal brotherhood, by teaching that all of humanity is a single tribe. This has doubtless been effective with some people. But enlarging one's tribe to include all of mankind is a stretch for the anti-conceptual mentality, and the dogmas of religion have more often been used to rationalize hostility toward people with different concrete practices, beliefs, aspirations, nationalities, etc.

Today, tolerance is grounded chiefly on the premise of relativism: the doctrine that there is no objective basis for judging people as good or bad, ideas as true or false, cultures as primitive or advanced. For the anti-conceptual mentality, indeed, relativism is the only possible escape route from tribal prejudice. The refusal to judge is the only alternative to judging by concrete-bound criteria. If one does not think in terms of principles, one has no way of distinguishing those aspects of human conduct and character that are subject to objective evaluation from those aspects that are optional. Whether someone is honest or dishonest, whether his skin is black or white, whether he believes in astral projections, whether he is married or single—it's all a matter of taste, just as, for the conventional tribal outlook, it's all subject to censure or approval by the tribe. The two outlooks are sides of the same anti-conceptual coin, equally irrational, equally unjust. There is little point in replacing mindless bigotry with mindless acceptance. The latter is hardly an Objectivist virtue, and cannot validly be classified under the same concept as the intellectual tolerance discussed above.

To be sure, there is a certain broad parallel between intellectual tolerance and the rational, benevolent attitude one should take toward human diversity. Just as one should not morally judge someone solely on the content of his ideas, so one should not judge someone for preferences or practices that are morally optional. That is a requirement of justice. In a more positive vein, we can treat diversity as a discovery mechanism akin to the intellectual process of discussion and debate. Within the boundaries set by the objective principles of a rational ethic, there is an enormous range of interests, tastes, habits, vocations, avocations, lifestyles, fashions, and forms of relationship that are possible to human beings and capable of creating value for their adherents.

As individuals, we cannot actualize more than a tiny fraction of this vast potential in our own lives and persons. One cannot have a definite identity without foreclosing some possibilities in order to pursue others. By interacting with those who have chosen different paths in life, we may learn something we can apply to our own lives, something we would not have learned from the neighbors next door. Diversity is a way of exploring the path not taken: we can experience vicariously a much wider range of the human potential that dwells within us. A person with the somewhat cautious reserve of an Anglo-Saxon upbringing, for example, might take special delight in the sexual energy of Mardi Gras, the exuberant elan of the French, the certainty of cabbies, the salt of Jewish humor.

A cosmopolitan interest in and acceptance of such diversity should therefore be recognized as an element of benevolence. But it cannot validly be described as *tolerance*. As I have noted, that concept presupposes an object with a negative value significance, which is not the case here. Intellectual tolerance is concerned with ideas we consider to be false—a negative attribute. But the differences we are discussing now fall within the range of the good, or at least the neutral. There is nothing for a white person to tolerate in one whose skin is black, because skin color has no value significance whatever. Describing the proper attitude toward people of different race or ethnicity as one of tolerance assumes that human beings naturally fear and resent such differences. It perpetuates the expectation that concrete-bound bigotry is natural, the to-be-expected, a kind of original sin that can be suppressed but never overcome.

Most people would find it bizarre to speak of tolerating blonds. For whatever reason, hair color has not been a basis of tribal identity or group politics in our culture; the concept of tolerance is never invoked in this context because there is too obviously nothing to tolerate. In a rational culture, the same would be true for race, ethnicity, and the like.

At best, therefore, the broader concept of tolerance attempts to integrate two things—the willingness to engage in discussion with intellectual opponents, and the cosmopolitan acceptance of diversity in lifestyle—that differ fundamentally. At worst, the term is a malignant anti-concept, an attempt to dignify relativism by allying it with something more honorable.[49] Intellectual tolerance was the product of a long and courageous battle for the freedom to seek the truth. It has nothing in common with the relativists' fear of taking a moral stand or their visceral hatred of standards of truth and achievement.

Notes

[1] Ayn Rand, *The Fountainhead* (1943; New York: Signet, 1952), p. 329. (Pagination in the Signet paperback editions of Rand's novels has changed with the most recent printing. Citations are to the most recent printing. Page numbers in older printings, where different, are given in brackets.)

[2] Ayn Rand, "The Ethics of Emergencies," in *The Virtue of Selfishness* (New York: New American Library, 1964).

[3] Cf. Lawrence A. Blum, *Friendship, Altruism and Morality* (London: Routledge and Kegan Paul, 1980), pp. 27, 75.

[4] Rand, "The Objectivist Ethics," in *The Virtue of Selfishness*, p. 27.

[5] Ayn Rand, "Faith and Force: The Destroyers of the Modern World," in *Philosophy: Who Needs It* (1982; New York: Signet, 1984), p. 61.

[6] Cf. Blum, *Friendship, Altruism and Morality*, p. 10.

[7] Rand, "The Ethics of Emergencies," p. 52.

[8] Ibid., p. 53.

[9] Ayn Rand, *Atlas Shrugged* (1957; New York: Signet, 1992), p. 614 [620-21].

[10] Among other memoirs of communist life, see Alex Kozinski, "The Dark Lessons of Utopia," *University of Chicago Law Review* 59 (1991), pp. 579-84.

[11] Nathaniel Branden, "Benevolence versus Altruism," *The Objectivist Newsletter*, July 1962, p. 28.

[12] See Rand, *Atlas Shrugged*, pp. 936-38 [945-47], and "The Objectivist Ethics," pp. 28-30. The virtues are rationality, independence, integrity, honesty, justice, productiveness, and pride.

[13] "Playboy Interview: Ayn Rand," *Playboy*, March 1964. See also Leonard Peikoff, *Objectivism: The Philosophy of Ayn Rand* (New York: Dutton, 1991), p. 239: "Extending help to others in such a context is an act of generosity, not an obligation. Nor is it an act that one may cherish as one's claim to virtue. Virtue, for Objectivism, consists in creating values, not in giving them away."

[14] Ayn Rand, "Philosophy and Sense of Life," in *The Romantic Manifesto*, 2nd rev. ed. (New York: Signet, 1975), p. 28.

[15] Rand, *Atlas Shrugged*, p. 113 [114-15].

[16] Rand, *The Fountainhead*, p. 363.

[17] This is my formulation of an argument discussed by Neera Kapur Badhwar ("The Virtues of Benevolence: The Unnamed Virtues in *The Fountainhead*," address given to the Ayn Rand Society, Dec. 1993.)

[18] Peikoff, *Objectivism: The Philosophy of Ayn Rand*, p. 342.

[19] Bertrand Russell, "Free Man's Worship," in *A New Introduction to Philosophy*, ed. Steven M. Cahn (New York: Harper & Row, 1971), pp. 333-34. See also Arthur Schopenhauer, *Essays and Aphorisms*, trans. R.J. Hollingdale (New York: Penguin, 1970), p. 50: "As a reliable compass for orientating yourself in life nothing is more useful than to accustom yourself to regarding this world as a place of atonement, a sort of penal colony. When you have done this you will order your expectations of life according to the nature of things and no longer regard the calamities, sufferings, torments and miseries of life as something irregular and not to be expected but will find them entirely in order, well knowing that each of us is here being punished for his existence and each in his own particular way.... The conviction that the world, and therefore man too, is something which really ought not to exist is in fact calculated to instill in us indulgence toward one another: for what can be expected of beings placed in such a situation as we are? From this point of view one might indeed consider that the appropriate form of address between man and man ought to be, not *monsieur, sir*, but *fellow sufferer, compagnon de misères*. However strange this may sound it ... reminds us of what are the most necessary of things: tolerance, patience, forbearance and charity, which each of us needs and which each of us therefore owes."

[20] Rand, "The Objectivist Ethics," p. 27. Rand characterizes virtue as a type of *action* rather than a habit or disposition, as Aristotle and most other philosophers have done. But I do not believe this represents a real difference in theory. Rand certainly recognized the reality of character as a disposition to act, but since a disposition is defined

by the action it disposes one to, that action is essential to understanding character. In relating virtue to value in this passage, moreover, Rand is stressing that virtue is a means, not its own reward; the difference between actions and dispositions is not relevant to this point.

[21] Note that in the account of the virtues in Galt's speech in *Atlas Shrugged*, pp. 936-38 [945-47], each paragraph begins with the formula, "X is the recognition of the fact that...."

[22] Rand, "The Objectivist Ethics," pp. 35-36.

[23] On the theory of visibility, see Rand, "The Objectivist Ethics," p. 35; and "Philosophy and Sense of Life," p. 32. The theory was developed in detail by Nathaniel Branden in *The Psychology of Self-Esteem* (1969; New York: Bantam, 1971), chap. 11, and *The Psychology of Romantic Love* (1980; New York: Bantam, 1981), chaps. 1-2. Branden uses the term "visibility" to refer specifically to the second of the two forms discussed in the text.

[24] I am speaking here of adults whose faculties are fully developed. Children, of course, are dependent on adults for food, shelter, and other forms of material wealth as well as for knowledge and education. It may also be that children cannot develop healthy self-esteem without some degree of parental love and support.

[25] Rand, "The Objectivist Ethics," pp. 34-35.

[26] Some of the benefits we receive from others satisfy condition (i) but not (ii). We benefit economically from the vast investments made by previous generations who obviously get nothing in return from us. We can learn things from other people without exchanging information—they may never have heard of us—or giving them any financial return by buying their books, etc. And we may be inspired by the example of someone who has never heard of us, and who therefore receives no reaffirmation of his values in exchange for what he gives us. All of these are examples of what economists call neighborhood effects. By their very nature, they are not instances of trade even in Rand's extended sense. Nevertheless, each of us is a source as well as a beneficiary of neighborhood effects, so there is a kind of metaphorical trade: we hold up our end in the mutual

interplay of unintended benefits. In addition, the greatest creators of knowledge and wealth (including artistic wealth) receive a return of visibility in the form of public recognition and honor. Finally, and most importantly, man does not live by neighborhood effects alone. They arise from the activity of deliberately producing values and seeking them from other people in specific exchanges, including personal, emotional ones. They are by-products of trade in Rand's sense, and thus do not refute the primacy of trade as the basic principle for human relationships.

27 Branden, *The Psychology of Self-Esteem*, p. 199.

28 Cf. Rand's letter to Isabel Paterson, May 8, 1948: "You explained to me that since every man is potentially capable of evil, this constitutes his Original Sin. I asked you why the same reasoning did not apply to man's good. Since every man is potentially capable of the highest virtues, why isn't he given credit for an Original Virtue?" *The Letters of Ayn Rand*, ed. Michael S. Berliner (New York: Dutton, 1995), p. 213.

29 Rand, *Atlas Shrugged*, p. 529 [535].

30 On the distinction between metaphysical and man-made facts, see Rand, "The Metaphysical and the Man-Made," in *Philosophy: Who Needs It.*

31 Rand, *The Fountainhead*, pp. 277, 293 [278, 293].

32 Badhwar, "The Virtues of Benevolence."

33 Rand, *The Fountainhead*, p. 573.

34 Ibid., p. 330.

35 Rand, *Atlas Shrugged*, p. 606 [612]. Ronald Merrill notes that this scene is especially revealing of Dagny's benevolence in light of her despair at this point in the novel. See *The Ideas of Ayn Rand* (La Salle, Ill.: Open Court, 1991), pp. 79-80.

36 *Random House Dictionary of the English Language*, 2nd ed. unabridged, s.v. "sympathy." See also Adam Smith, *Theory of Moral Sentiments*, ed. D. D. Raphael and A. L. Macfie (Oxford: Clarendon Press, 1976), 10 [I, i, i, 5].

37 Rand, *Atlas Shrugged*, p. 41 [47].

38 Peikoff, *Objectivism: The Philosophy of Ayn Rand*, p. 239.

[39] Rand, *Atlas Shrugged,* p. 606 [612].

[40] Ibid., p. 338 [342].

[41] Rand, *The Fountainhead,* p. 90.

[42] Cf. Roger Donway, "Beyond TANSTAAFL," *IOS Journal,* Vol. 5, #1 (April, 1995).

[43] David Kelley, *Truth and Toleration* (privately printed, 1990). Available from the Institute for Objectivist Studies.

[44] Ibid., p. 49.

[45] Ibid., p. 55.

[46] Tolerance in the sense I have defined it *does* extend to action in one straightforward sense. If a person acts on the basis of an idea that is false but not the product of irrationality, then we cannot condemn him for the action any more than for the idea itself. On the contrary, it would be a compromise of his integrity *not* to act on the basis of his convictions. If the convictions are false, the actions may well be destructive to the person himself or to others, and we may certainly oppose the action for that reason. But we cannot judge the person himself immoral for taking the action. It is for this reason, to take a fictional example, that the strikers in *Atlas Shrugged* do not condemn Dagny for failing to join them, even though they believe she is wrong in her position and consequently acting in a way that makes her an enemy. This is an issue of justice, however, not of benevolence per se; and it is distinct from the issues discussed in the text below.

[47] Ayn Rand, "The Missing Link," in *Philosophy: Who Needs It,* p. 38.

[48] Ibid., p. 39.

[49] On the nature of anti-concepts, see Ayn Rand, "'Extremism,' or The Art of Smearing," in *Capitalism: The Unknown Ideal* (New York: Signet, 1967).

About the Author

David Kelley, Ph.D., founder and executive director of the Institute for Objectivist Studies, is a professional philosopher, teacher, and writer. After earning a Ph.D. in philosophy from Princeton University in 1975, he joined the philosophy department of Vassar College, where he remained until 1984. While at Vassar, he taught a wide variety of courses at all levels, helped form Vassar's Cognitive Science Program, and served on the curriculum committee. He left Vassar in 1984 to work as an independent scholar and writer. During the academic year 1989-90, he taught at Brandeis University as a Visiting Lecturer.

Dr. Kelley's philosophical writings include *The Evidence of the Senses*, a detailed presentation of the Objectivist theory of perception; *The Art of Reasoning*, a widely used college logic textbook; and *Truth and Toleration*, an essay on the principles of intellectual exchange. He has published articles, and addressed philosophical organizations, on concept-formation, property rights, and many other topics. With Roger Donway, he co-authored *Laissez-Parler: Freedom in the Electronic Media*, a critique of government regulation. His articles on social issues and public policy have appeared in *Barrons, Harpers, The Sciences, Harvard Business Review, The Freeman, On Principle,* and elsewhere.

An active proponent of Objectivism for over 20 years, he has been a leading intellectual figure in the Objectivist and classical liberal movements. He has given lectures at Harvard, Yale, Berkeley, Amherst, and many other colleges and universities. He has also addressed the Mont Pelerin Society, the Free Press Association, the Cato Institute Summer Seminar, as well as many Objectivist conferences.

Institute for Objectivist Studies

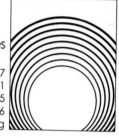

82 Washington Street, Suite 207
Poughkeepsie, New York 12601
(914) 471-6100 Fax (914) 471-6195
Toll-free: 1-800-374-1776
E-mail: ios@ios.org WWW: http://ios.org

Founded in early 1990, the Institute for Objectivist Studies has become a widely recognized center for research and education on Objectivism, the philosophy originated by Ayn Rand, author of *The Fountainhead, Atlas Shrugged,* and other works of fiction and nonfiction. Objectivism is a secular world view that stresses reason, individualism, respect for achievement, and liberty.

Serving students, scholars, and the public at large, the Institute's programs and activities include seminars and courses, original research projects, and a newsletter. The Institute also acts as a clearinghouse for information about Objectivism.

As an educational organization, the Institute encourages the exploration of ideas in an atmosphere of free and open discussion.

Support for Institute programs comes from activity fees, grants from foundations and corporations, and individual contributions from Institute members. The United States Internal Revenue Service has designated the Institute a tax-exempt, 501(c)(3) educational organization.

For more information, write to IOS at the address above, visit our home page on the World Wide Web (http://ios.org), or call 1-800-374-1776.